ESSENTIAL DK MANAGERS

NEGOT
SKILLS

H662

TIM HINDLE

DK PUBLISHING,

A DK PUBLISHING BOOK

Project Editor Sasha Heseltine
Project Art Editor Ellen Woodward
Editor Marian Broderick
US Editor Ray Rogers
Designers Elaine C. Monaghan, Austin Barlow
Assistant Editor Felicity Crowe
Assistant Designer Laura Watson

DTP Designer Jason Little
Production Controller Alison Jones

Series Editor Jane Simmonds
Series Art Editor Jayne Jones

Managing Editor Stephanie Jackson
Managing Art Editor Nigel Duffield

First American Edition, 1998
2 4 6 8 10 9 7 5 3 1

Published in the United States by
DK Publishing, Inc.
95 Madison Avenue
New York, New York 10016

Visit us on the World Wide Web at
http://www.dk.com

Library of Congress Cataloging-in-Publication Data
Negotiating Skills. -- 1st American ed.
p. cm. -- (Essential Managers)
Includes index.
ISBN 0-7894-2448-7
1. Negotiation. 2. Persuasion (Psychology).
3. Negotiation in business. I. DK Publishing, Inc.
II. Series.
BF637.N4N424 1998   97-38889
158.5--DC21   CIP

Reproduced by Colourscan, Singapore
Printed and bound in Italy by Graphicom srl

CONTENTS

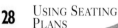

CONDUCTING A
NEGOTIATION

CLOSING A
NEGOTIATION

INTRODUCTION

Negotiation involves parties, who each have something that the other wants, reaching an agreement to exchange through a process of bargaining. *Negotiating Skills* explains this principle of exchange and gives you the confidence and skill to conduct negotiations and achieve a mutually acceptable outcome. Designed for easy access to relevant information, including 101 practical tips, the book covers the whole process of negotiation, from preparation to closing the deal, and is suitable for novices and seasoned negotiators alike. It includes essential information on how to devise a strategy, how to make concessions, what to do when negotiations break down, and how to make use of third parties to resolve deadlock and conflict.

PREPARING FOR A NEGOTIATION

To negotiate successfully you need a game plan – your ultimate aim and a strategy for achieving it. Prepare thoroughly before a negotiation to facilitate the success of your game plan.

DEFINING NEGOTIATION

Negotiation occurs when someone else has what you want and you are prepared to bargain for it – and vice versa. Negotiations take place every day between family members, with shopkeepers, and – almost continuously – in the workplace.

1 To become a good negotiator, learn to "read" the other party's needs.

2 Bear in mind that it is almost impossible for a negotiator to do too much preparation.

UNDERSTANDING THE PRINCIPLES

Successful negotiating – an attempt by two people to achieve a mutually acceptable solution – should not result in a winner and a loser. It is a process that ends either with a satisfying conclusion for both sides (win/win), or with failure for both sides (lose/lose). The art of negotiation is based on attempting to reconcile what constitutes a good result for you with what constitutes a good result for the other party. To achieve a situation where both sides win something, you need to be well prepared, alert, and flexible.

RECOGNIZING THE SKILLS

Negotiation is a skill that anyone can learn, and there are plenty of opportunities to practice it once learned. The core skills required for successful negotiations include:

- The ability to define a range of objectives, yet be flexible about some of them;
- The ability to explore the possibilities of a wide range of options;
- The ability to prepare well;
- Interactive competence, the ability to listen to and question other parties; and
- The ability to prioritize clearly.

These proficiencies are useful in everyday life as well as in negotiations. By taking the time to learn them, you will be able to enhance more than just your bargaining abilities.

3 Start by visualizing possible gains, not losses.

4 Practice negotiating to improve upon your skills.

▼ STUDYING NEGOTIATION
At the start of a commercial negotiation, two teams face each other around a table. Note how each team member's body language is supportive of their partner.

TEAM A

Head is tilted toward partner

TEAM B

Body leans toward partner

Eye contact is maintained with partner

CATEGORIZING TYPES

Different negotiation types require different skills. In business and commerce, each instance of negotiation displays certain characteristics. It may be formal or informal, ongoing or a one-off, depending on who is negotiating for what. The parties involved in a business – such as employees, shareholders, trade unions, management, suppliers, customers, and the government – all have different interests and individual points of view. Whichever group you belong to, you need to reconcile such differences through negotiation: for example, shareholders negotiate with boards of directors over company strategy, unions negotiate with employers over pay and conditions, and governments negotiate with accountants over taxation.

5 Be prepared to compromise when you negotiate.

6 Determine your strategy according to the type of negotiation.

TYPES OF NEGOTIATION IN ORGANIZATIONS

TYPES	EXAMPLES	PARTIES INVOLVED
DAY-TO-DAY/ MANAGERIAL Such negotiations concern internal problems and the working relationship between groups of employees.	● Arranging pay, terms, and working conditions. ● Defining job roles and areas of responsibility. ● Increasing output via, for example, more overtime.	● Management ● Subordinates ● Colleagues ● Trade unions ● Legal advisers
COMMERCIAL The driving factor in these negotiations, which take place between an organization and an external party, is usually financial gain.	● Winning a contract to supply customers. ● Scheduling the delivery of goods and services. ● Agreeing on the quality and price of products.	● Management ● Suppliers ● Customers ● Government ● Trade unions ● Legal advisers
LEGAL These negotiations are usually formal and legally binding. Disputes over precedents can become as significant as the main issues.	● Complying with local authority and national planning laws. ● Communicating with regulators (such as antitrust authorities).	● Local government ● National government ● Regulators ● Management

APPOINTING AGENTS

John F. Kennedy, US President, once said, "Let us never negotiate out of fear, but let us never fear to negotiate." In reality, of course, you may be reluctant to negotiate because you are afraid of an unfamiliar process. If this is the case, you can find someone to negotiate for you. Such people are known as "agents," and they can be assigned as much or as little responsibility as you, the "principal" who employs them, wish to give them in a given negotiation. However, you should always clearly lay out the full extent of that responsibility in advance of the negotiation.

Some common examples of agents include trade union members, who negotiate as agents on behalf of employees, and lawyers, who often negotiate as agents on behalf of all types of stakeholder in an organization, including management, shareholders, and customers.

7 Define an agent's responsibilites very clearly.

POINTS TO REMEMBER

● When negotiating, you need to know where you are prepared to give ground – or not.

● A matter under negotiation may be intangible, and therefore must be defined before negotiation can proceed.

● Negotiation implies that you are willing to compromise on the issue under discussion.

● Anything that applies to you as a negotiator applies to the person with whom you are negotiating.

NEGOTIATING IN DAILY LIFE

Domestic situations often involve negotiation. For example, you may agree to take your neighbor's children to school every Monday and Thursday if they take yours on Tuesday and Friday, and you each do alternate Wednesdays. On occasion, negotiated terms may need to be renegotiated. For example, you may have negotiated a price for one vase in a bazaar, but if you buy more than one vase, you should be in a position to renegotiate for a lower price on the first vase. When making an offer on a house, you may need to raise your offer and renegotiate terms if someone else is interested.

▲ **NEGOTIATING WITH REALTORS**
If you are considering buying a house, you will need to discuss terms and conditions of the purchase with a realtor.

UNDERSTANDING THE PRINCIPLE OF EXCHANGE

With a proper understanding of all the processes involved (preparation, proposal, debate, bargaining, and closing), negotiating can create a successful outcome for all parties. Central to this is the principle of exchange: you must give in order to receive.

8 Clarify your priorities: be ready to concede less important points.

STAGES OF NEGOTIATION

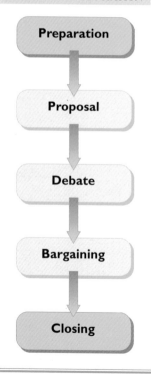

Preparation

Proposal

Debate

Bargaining

Closing

WINNING ON EACH SIDE

The key to negotiation is to realize that all parties need to gain something of value in exchange for any concessions they make. Only then can they all come away feeling successful. Try to achieve this by understanding that what is valued by your party may not be valued by the other. Whereas in a competitive sport victory is valued by both parties – so if one side wins, the other loses – negotiations, in contrast, can end in a win/win conclusion. When trade unions negotiate with a company's management, they may gain more pay for their members, while the management may gain assurances about increased productivity.

CULTURAL DIFFERENCES

Different cultures approach negotiations in very different ways. For example, Europeans and Americans often find the Japanese reluctance to engage in outright confrontation confusing or ambiguous. On the other hand, the Japanese find apparently unequivocal statements or viewpoints unsubtle and difficult to work into a compromise.

BEING FLEXIBLE

Flexibility is a vital characteristic around any negotiating table. The balance of power between the parties fluctuates as negotiations progress. For example, if you are bargaining in a market over a souvenir, you may become less enthusiastic when you discover that the vendor is not able to deliver to your home – anything you buy, you are going to have to take away with you. The vendor should be alert to any such loss of interest, and, in this case, you can expect them to lower their price in order to compensate and to keep you interested.

9 Be flexible – it is a sign of strength, not of weakness.

10 If you agree in haste, you may repent at leisure.

CASE STUDY

Freelance architect John was short of work when Bill, a property developer, asked him to draw up some plans for a warehouse that he was developing on a valuable site. John agreed, and Bill, seeing John was eager to work, offered him half his normal rate of pay. John objected but eventually agreed to do the work for about 60% of his usual rate. It was dull, boring work and involved long trips.

Both parties thought Bill had won and John had lost. After a few weeks, John got a big new contract and began to resent Bill's job. He would do the work in a hurry at the end of the day when he was tired.

When finished, the warehouse had an awkward leak, perhaps the result of John's half-hearted effort. Bill tried unsuccessfully to fix it cheaply. Customers were few, and Bill closed the warehouse after three years.

◀ **EXCHANGING UNSUCCESSFULLY**
In this situation, negotiations led at the beginning to an apparent winner and an apparent loser. However, over time, these positions became reversed as John, the supposed loser, ended up ahead while Bill, the apparent winner, realized that he made an expensive mistake by trying to save money at the outset.

NEGOTIATING A ▶ FAIR EXCHANGE
Both parties in this case can be said to have won. Juan was aware that no more hard cash would be offered by the software company, so they joined in an alliance. Both parties achieved their common aim, which was to minimize their loss if the venture failed and to maximize their profits if it succeeded.

CASE STUDY

Juan was a computer software designer with an idea for a new computer game that he believed would be hugely successful. However, it would take a long time to program it, and he needed to earn a living in the meantime.

He went to see his friend Ellen, an executive at a large computer company. Ellen and her colleagues liked the idea, but offered Juan only $10,000. Juan said it would take him

nine months to develop the game, and, while $10,000 would enable him to survive, it was not sufficient reward.

He suggested that the $10,000 should act as an advance on future profits, and that he and the company share the profits in the ratio 25:75. Eventually, a 20:80 split was agreed upon. The game was launched with a big marketing campaign and was a huge success, making both parties a lot of money.

IDENTIFYING OBJECTIVES

The first step in planning any form of negotiation is to identify all your objectives. What do you want to get out of the negotiation? Only when you know the answers can you begin to create a plan that will enable you to achieve these goals.

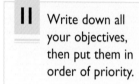

11 Write down all your objectives, then put them in order of priority.

CLARIFYING OBJECTIVES

There is rarely just one objective to a negotiation. You may be buying a chess set in a foreign country, but you also want to take it back to your home country without paying duty and you want to pay by credit card. Therefore, buying the chess set is not your sole objective. Similarly, when unions are negotiating for a pay raise for their members, they may also be looking to reduce excessive working hours or to improve the rate that members will be paid for working at weekends.

Before entering a negotiation, make a list of all your objectives, then put them in your order of priority and identify those that you can live without. When it comes to compromise, you will be aware of which objectives to yield first.

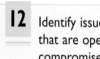

12 Identify issues that are open to compromise and those that are not.

13 Express each objective in a single sentence.

ASSIGNING DIFFERENT PRIORITIES

FOR COMPANY	PRIORITY	FOR SUPPLIER
Price	First	Quality
Time	Second	Price
Quality	Third	Time
Quantity	Fourth	Quantity

CLASSIFYING PRIORITIES

Divide your priorities into three groups:
● Those that are your ideal;
● Those that represent a realistic target;
● Those that are the minimum you must fulfill to feel that the negotiation has not been a failure.

Assign each of them a value. For example, if buying a chess set is your prime objective, give it a value of ten. Paying by credit card may be something that you can yield on, so give it a lower value of two. Finding the chess set in marble may not be crucial but still have a value of, say, seven. Prioritizing in this way ensures that you do not end up compromising on the wrong issues.

14 Abandon any totally unrealistic objectives before you negotiate.

ASSESSING ▶ PRIORITIES

In Anil's case, a decent pension was more important than the other assets of the job; on GUT's side, the expense and trouble of changing the pension fund outstripped the benefits of gaining a talented recruit.

CASE STUDY

Anil was about to accept a new job with Great Universal Technology, who offered him an increased salary and relocation. The only drawback was that GUT, without explanation, said that it was not prepared to include him in its company pension plan but would pay a comparable sum into a new pension plan that he took out on his own.

He talked to an accountant and discovered that he would lose out by starting a new fund in this way. Thinking that GUT would be accommodating, he insisted that it sign him on to its own pension plan.

GUT withdrew its job offer, saying that to accommodate him would have involved changing the pension plan of everybody else in the company, and that it was not prepared to do this. The negotiation broke down because GUT had not explained the problem fully.

DISTINGUISHING BETWEEN WANTS AND NEEDS

A useful distinction that can help in assigning values to different objectives is that between "wants" and "needs." On the one hand, you may decide that you would like to replace your basic telephone with a sophisticated new telephone with lots of automatic functions. On the other hand, when your computer hard drive breaks down irretrievably, you need that replaced as soon as possible to be able to function properly in the office. So, while you *want* a new phone, you do not need one. What you *need* is a computer hard drive. Understanding the subtlety of this difference is vital to recognizing your opponent's wants and needs around the negotiating table.

PREPARING YOURSELF

Preparing yourself for serious negotiation involves thorough research. You will need to seek out useful information to support your objectives – once you have identified them – and find information that will help you to undermine the other party's case.

15 Be sure to gather all key information relevant to a negotiation.

USING PREPARATION TIME

Allowing for preparation time before you start negotiating is vital, as is the constructive use of that time. Allow yourself enough time to complete your research satisfactorily. You may need time to find statistics and case studies to support your arguments and thumbnail sketches of the personalities with whom you will be negotiating. Absorb this information, and use it tactically. For example, if you plan to use complex statistics, prepare an explanation to show how they support your case, rather than undermine the other party by exposing their ignorance of your material.

ASSEMBLING DATA

One valuable use of your preparation time is to acquire in-depth information about the people you will be dealing with and their business. This will be available from both electronic and paper-based sources. Visit a library; search the Internet; talk to others who know the people with whom you are about to negotiate. Look at the company's annual reports, at market research, and at old press releases. A careful scan of such sources can help you come up with telling arguments to support your case, but be absolutely certain of the accuracy of the information you have gleaned.

▲ ASSEMBLING DOCUMENTS

Arrange your data so it is easily accessible. Photocopy key pages of text; use colored pens to highlight points. Time spent checking data is not wasted.

DEVELOPING LOGIC

Having compiled plenty of data, begin to develop a logical argument. You will need to follow through your logic in one of two basic ways:

- Deductively – a conclusion follows from a set of premises. For example, "I am a shareholder in Great Universal Technology. GUT will pay a dividend this quarter of 50 cents per share. Therefore I shall receive a dividend of 50 cents per share this quarter."
- Inductively – a conclusion is drawn from examples based on experience. For example, "Every time someone in GUT has become vice president, they have received a pay raise. I am being made vice president, therefore I will receive a pay raise." If the expected pay raise fails to follow promotion on just one occasion, it undermines the logic.

16 Sit in as an observer on other people's negotiations.

17 Learn tactics from the biographies of famous negotiators.

ANTICIPATING POSSIBLE DIRECTIONS OF A NEGOTIATION

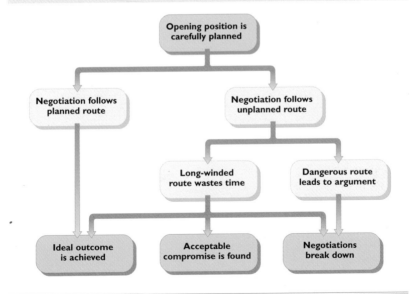

Opening position is carefully planned

Negotiation follows planned route

Negotiation follows unplanned route

Long-winded route wastes time

Dangerous route leads to argument

Ideal outcome is achieved

Acceptable compromise is found

Negotiations break down

ASSESSING THE OPPOSITION

When preparing your case, it is to your advantage to study the likely strengths and weaknesses of the opposition's negotiating position and to research the background of the individuals who are doing the negotiating. Find out about their negotiating histories.

18 Talk to people who know the other party in the negotiations.

QUESTIONS TO ASK YOURSELF

Q Does the opposition have experienced negotiators?

Q Are there any differences in opinion within the opposition?

Q Does the opposition have the knowledge and facts necessary to achieve its aims?

Q Does the opposition have the power and authority to achieve its aims?

Q Is the opposition under pressure to settle quickly?

LOOKING AT THEIR CASE

Study the opposition's case in the round – that is, look at all aspects of their case. It will have strengths and weaknesses. Aim to expose its major weaknesses in order to undermine its strengths.

Although the logical argument in favor of the opposition's case may be strong, you may be able to counter a logical proposition with, say, a moral objection. For example, if a fish farm wants to use a new type of feed that makes the fish grow 15 percent more rapidly, look for any repercussions of such a fast weight gain. Research may show that the feed makes the bones of the fish so weak that they can barely swim.

ASSESSING STRENGTHS

Since negotiation involves a process of gradual convergence toward agreement or compromise, you need to assess the opposition's starting point and their strengths. Do they have a strong case? Is it logical? Is it morally acceptable? Do they have a strong leader with good negotiating skills? Once you have an idea of the opposition's strong points, assess in what direction they might go once you begin to bargain. How much room do they have to negotiate? Would an adjournment work in their favor, for example, should they want to consult with a higher authority?

19 Be aware that the opposition might have a hidden agenda.

IDENTIFYING OBJECTIVES

Try to identify the opposition's objectives – just as you have identified your own. Make a list of their supposed objectives, and prioritize them. Categorize them according to whether you think they are top, middle, or low priority. Remember that these judgments can only be guesswork and that they need to be tested by observation as the negotiations proceed.

GUESSING AT THE OPPOSITION'S OBJECTIVES

TOP PRIORITY
These are the objectives that you think the opposition considers as vital to achieve.

MIDDLE PRIORITY
These are the objectives that you think the opposition would like to achieve.

LOW PRIORITY
These are the objectives that you think the opposition would regard as bonuses if achieved.

ANALYZING THEIR WEAKNESSES

Just as you need to understand the opposition's strengths, you also must be aware of their weaknesses – both of their case and of their individual skills. For instance, if the opposition consists of a group of people, analyze whether there is any scope to divide and conquer – say, by yielding one point that you know will please some of them but displease others. Research weaknesses in their arguments in advance by looking for morally or politically problematic areas in their case that you could fully exploit. For example, a motion by the sales director of an electrical goods wholesaler to sell off at a high discount some damaged electrical goods raises various ethical and legal problems that could be exploited.

USING FORMAL SOURCES OF INFORMATION

Carefully examine all formal written information about your opponents. For example, analyze articles printed in trade journals and other allied publications that detail what they have done. They may include invaluable background information about your opponent's present state, history, and current strategic objectives. You can also examine all of the publicly available documentation held by government agencies about an opponent's legal history and financial circumstances.

20 Keep testing your own assessment of the opposition against the way they behave during the negotiations.

LEARNING FROM EARLIER ENCOUNTERS

Negotiations often take place between parties who have already dealt with each other over similar issues, such as suppliers renegotiating an annually renewed contract or employees negotiating changes in their terms of employment. If you are negotiating with a known party, analyze the way previous negotiations were handled. Reexamine old minutes or notes and consult with any of your colleagues who were present. Reshape your tactics accordingly, but remember that as you become more familiar with the opposition's modus operandi, so they will be formulating objectives in line with their knowledge of your previous strategies.

POINTS TO REMEMBER

- The balance of power in earlier negotiations may not be the same as it is in the current round.
- The opposing negotiator may have a new job with more authority and more power.
- An opposing negotiator's new job may expose new weaknesses along with strengths.
- The time pressures for both teams may be different.
- The amount of preparation done by each party may be different in any round of a negotiation.

21 If possible, always consult with any members of a previous negotiating team.

22 Research in advance who will be representing the opposition.

FINDING COMMON GROUND

Negotiation involves mapping out ways of finding common ground for agreement or compromise. This goal may be achieved more readily by parties who have previously negotiated and are more likely to understand the concessions that the other side may be willing to make.

For example, if an employee approaches a manager wanting to negotiate a salary increase, he or she may find that the manager's budgetary constraints or a general company ruling prohibit any direct salary increases that year. However, instead of a direct monthly increase, the employee and the manager could discuss and agree on alternative ways of settling on a financial reward that would circumvent these constraints. Both parties could agree on an extra week of annual leave, for example, as an alternative to a pay raise. Such a flexible attitude being shown by both parties, as well as the willingness to seek out common ground, can result in an appropriate compromise being made.

Negotiating with More Than One Group

When the opposition consists of more than one interest group, you should assess whether there are any conflicts between these parties as well as assessing each group and individual as you would normally. Additionally, identify who has the power to make important decisions on behalf of the various groups. If, for example, you are the bidder in a corporate takeover, start by negotiating with the shareholders. In situations where a government body is involved, use a different strategy: address the wider effects of a takeover and use a team that includes lawyers to negotiate and examine all the implications.

Cultural Differences

Cultural differences exist between races, age groups, and sexes, and you may be able to use these to your advantage. If your opponent is a middle-aged Russian, for example, you may imply that he or she lacks experience of commercial markets. Similarly, a well-educated but young American might be accused of lack of relevant work experience.

Using Informal Sources of Information

To be proficient at gathering information you must train yourself to think like a detective. Use informal social occasions, business networks, casual encounters, or timely phone calls to the appropriate people to find out how your opponents operate on a day-to-day basis. You can also send someone to their offices to see how they treat their staff and their customers, or invite one of

their long-standing customers to lunch and ask a few discreet questions. Disenchanted ex-employees can also prove to be a mine of useful information, but beware in case they are unwittingly passing on to you misinformation with little basis in reality.

COLLECTING ▶ INFORMATION
Use an informal social occasion with someone who has connections with both parties in the negotiations to acquire as much information about your opponents and their strategies as possible.

CHOOSING A STRATEGY

Once you are clear about your objectives and have analyzed your opponents' probable objectives, you should be ready to formulate a strategy for achieving your ends. Use the strengths of the personalities in your team to devise your strategy.

23 Always keep your negotiating strategy simple and flexible.

QUESTIONS TO ASK YOURSELF

Q How will you decide on a strategy and tactics?

Q How many people do you need in your negotiating team?

Q How long will it take you to formulate a strategy?

Q Do all team members need to attend all the negotiations?

Q When can you rehearse your roles and tactics?

CONSIDERING OBJECTIVES

A strategy is an overall policy designed to achieve a number of specified objectives. It is not to be confused with tactics, which are the detailed methods used to carry out a strategy.

Your strategy will depend on several factors including personality, circumstance, and the issue under negotiation. Look carefully at the dynamics of the members of your team in relation to the reasons for and subject of the negotiation, and choose players whose combined strengths and skills can best achieve the team's objectives.

UNDERSTANDING ROLES

Just as every football team needs a quarterback, so every negotiating team requires certain "classic" roles to be filled in order to conclude negotiations successfully. These roles include the Leader, Good Guy, Bad Guy, Hard Liner, and Sweeper. Other roles can also be adopted to suit the circumstances of each particular negotiation you are involved in.

The ideal negotiating team should have between three and five members, and all the key roles should be represented. It is not essential, however, for every role to be filled by a single person – it is common for individual team members to adopt a number of roles that complement each other and reflect their own character traits.

24 Hide short tempers and frustration when negotiating, and never walk out in a rage.

DEFINING ROLES WITHIN TEAMS

ROLES

RESPONSIBILITIES

LEADER
Any negotiating team needs a leader. This may be the person with the most expertise, not necessarily the most senior member of the team.

- Conducting the negotiation, calling on others occasionally when needed.
- Ruling on matters of expertise – for example, deciding if there is enough money available to finance a takeover bid.
- Orchestrating the other members of the team.

GOOD GUY
This is the person with whom most members of the opposing team will identify. They may wish that the Good Guy was their only opponent.

- Expressing sympathy and understanding for the opposition's point of view.
- Appearing to backtrack on a position previously held by their own team.
- Lulling the members of the opposing team into a false sense of security, allowing them to relax.

BAD GUY
The opposite of the Good Guy, this person's role is to make the opposition feel that agreement could be more easily reached without him or her.

- Stopping the negotiations from proceeding, if and when needed.
- Undermining any argument or point of view the opposition puts forward.
- Intimidating the opposition and trying to expose their weaknesses.

HARD LINER
This member takes a tough line on everything. He or she presents the opposition with complications and is often deferred to by team members.

- Delaying progress by using stalling tactics.
- Allowing others to retreat from soft offers that they might have made.
- Observing and recording the progress of the negotiations.
- Keeping the team focused on the objectives of the negotiations.

SWEEPER
This person picks up and brings together all the points of view expressed and then puts them forward as a single cogent case.

- Suggesting ways or tactics to get out of a deadlocked negotiation.
- Preventing the discussion from straying too far from the main issues.
- Pointing out any inconsistencies in the opposition's argument.

ASSIGNING ROLES

In negotiation, good strategy involves the appropriate deployment of personnel. You must decide on the roles and responsibilities that you want your team members to assume. Are they better at observing and listening than talking? Have they met any of the opposition before? Are they extroverted? An extroverted member of your team could, for example, play the role of the Good Guy. Allocate roles carefully, since your team must be able to tackle any moves made by the opposition.

25 Draw up a written schedule of times for briefings and rehearsing tactics.

▼ **REHEARSING ROLES**
When you have selected your team, gather them together for a rehearsal, each member playing out their role. Resolve any gaps or duplication of roles in the team.

Practice using visual aids

Encourage note-taking for reference during the real negotiations

THE IMPORTANCE OF APPEARANCE

Carefully consider your appearance in advance – first impressions count for a lot. Think about the type of negotiation you are entering, and dress accordingly. Power dressing can influence the way that people perceive you and your authority, but it can carry negative connotations of aggression. Encourage your team to dress in the same way, and if you want to appear formal, wear a jacket when you arrive. If in doubt, dress conservatively.

26 Wear clothes that you find comfortable but which are smart and fairly conservative.

BRIEFING YOUR TEAM

In order for members of your negotiating team to play particular roles successfully, you must brief them thoroughly. Avoid sending out contradictory messages during negotiations by keeping absent members up to date. For example, if the Leader claims early on that he or she has full authority to agree on a price, make sure that the Hard Liner does not come into the meeting later and, in an attempt to stall for time, assert that head office will need to be consulted for approval on the price. Such an inconsistency can seriously undermine the credibility of your team.

As well as encouraging individual preparation, make sure that the complete team is present for at least one dress rehearsal that uses actual data and visual material where possible. Take notes that can be used afterward to analyze how the team can improve their strategies and tactics.

27 Practice being silent around a negotiating table.

CASE STUDY

Beth and Kurt were sent to Hong Kong by their employer, an electronics company, to persuade a manufacturer to buy some of its microchips.

Before they left, they rehearsed a number of good arguments and decided that Beth was to make the case. In Hong Kong, the factory managers approved of the proposal and seemed happy. However, while Beth was talking, Kurt overheard someone say that "Westerners never accept the first price offered." So when the Chinese put forward their price, expecting it to be rejected, Kurt interrupted.

Beth was taken aback, since she thought that the offer price was perfectly reasonable. However, she was pleased to have been interrupted when the Chinese agreed to a price 10% higher than their original offer. Both sides departed happy with the deal.

◄ WORKING TOGETHER

In this example of teamwork, Beth was acting as the Leader and Kurt fulfilled the other roles. It would have been much more difficult for a single negotiator, working on his or her own, to have picked up sufficient information to clinch this deal as successfully.

USING AN AGENDA

In certain types of negotiation, it is helpful to draw up an agenda – a written list of issues to be debated. Use an agenda to gain agreement from all the participants, before the negotiating begins, on the areas that are to be discussed or left out altogether.

28 Try to set the agenda – it will influence the rest of the meeting.

POINTS TO REMEMBER

- Items should be allocated a fixed period of time on an agenda.
- A draft agenda should be sent to all parties in advance.
- Typed agendas should have wide margins for making notes.
- Supplementary papers should be distributed with an agenda.
- Agendas can be so important that sometimes their content needs to be negotiated.

DRAFTING AN AGENDA

The items to be discussed on an agenda can become a central part of negotiating strategy, through both the order in which they are to be considered and the time that is given to each. It is therefore sometimes necessary to hold extensive discussions in order to draft an agenda before negotiations begin. Bear in mind when drafting an agenda that it should:
- Formally define what the discussion is about;
- Informally influence the substance of the discussion by prioritizing issues.

◄ WRITING AN AGENDA
An agenda helps to focus a negotiation on its aims and objectives. Since negotiation is not about airing grievances but achieving solutions, headings should use unchallenging and nonspecific language.

Termination Negotiations
July 24th, 9:00 a.m.
Board Room

1. (9:00) Read minutes of previous meeting.
2. (9:15) Management consultants present case.
3. (9:45) Personnel Director presents case.
   (10:15) Coffee break.
4. (10:30) Financial Director presents case.
5. (11:00) Summing up by Managing Director.
6. (11:30) Discussion.
7. (12:30) Close.

Details of meeting head agenda

Previous decisions are ratified

First speaker sets tone

Specialist participant provides detailed information

Scheduled times

Close of meeting is indicated

AGREEING TO AN AGENDA

If you receive an agenda from the other party, analyze it and adjust your strategy accordingly. The party that sets the agenda is the party with the greatest interest in the meeting and will usually claim the first speaking slot. Thus, you may wish to rearrange the order of speakers to your advantage. If an agenda is relayed to you by phone, ensure you are not thrown off by the informality. Absorb all the information and consult the opposition about changes you wish to make.

29 Arrive a little early for meetings so you will look efficient and relaxed.

30 Write an agenda in simple language, and include timings for each of the issues under discussion.

SCHEDULING AGENDAS

In some negotiations, a time limit is imposed due to the busy schedules of the people involved. Other negotiations require the parties involved to sit around a table for as long as it takes to reach agreement (in the case of peace treaties, for instance, or of juries in courts of law). Always set a target time for the meeting to end, and schedule the discussion to fit within that time constraint. Remember that most people will become irritable if a meeting overruns its schedule.

RECORDING INFORMATION

Negotiation inevitably involves making concessions that a negotiating team might regret (or at least have second thoughts about). Thus, many people like to record the proceedings on audio cassette. This can be problematic, however, for a number of reasons: it can be difficult to position a tape recorder to pick up all the dialogue; vital parts of the discussion may also be lost if batteries have to be changed; and cassettes rarely last the duration of a negotiation.

If you want to record the meeting in this way, obtain the agreement of the other party in advance. In addition to tape recordings, experienced negotiators always ensure that detailed written minutes of the proceedings are taken.

TAKING NOTES ▶
Use a recorder to take down comments or notes quickly and easily.

CREATING THE RIGHT ATMOSPHERE

The outcome of a negotiating session can be influenced by the environment in which it is held. Create a positive atmosphere for opposing teams from the outset of the proceedings by making the location suitable for the size and nature of the occasion.

31 Do not run a negotiation longer than two hours without a break.

DECIDING ON LOCATION

There are many considerations to take into account when selecting a location, including convenience, neutrality, and facilities. Do you require audio-visual aids or flip charts? Do you need to rent them, and from whom? How long are the facilities reserved? Can you stay overnight nearby if agreement is not reached within one day? Choose a location that fulfills as many of your requirements as possible.

32 Keep a clock on the wall so that everybody can see what time it is.

TYPES OF LOCATION FOR NEGOTIATIONS

LOCATION	FACTORS TO CONSIDER
HOME GROUND An office or room in your company building is considered home territory.	● It is easy for you to organize strategic interruptions. ● It is difficult to avoid unplanned interruptions. ● It is easy to call on your own in-house experts for relevant contributions to the negotiations.
NEUTRAL GROUND The office of a third party, or a rented public room, is considered neutral ground.	● Neither party gains the upper hand because of their familiarity with the location. ● Both sides need to "ship in" their experts and any background material they might require.
AWAY GROUND Away ground is an office or room belonging to the other negotiating party.	● Lack of familiarity with the surroundings can be disturbing. ● You have no control of the logistics. ● You can procrastinate by saying that you need to refer the matter back to someone in your office.

ATTENDING TO DETAILS

When hosting a negotiation, take complete control of the situation: manipulate the atmosphere, timing, and the nature of the breaks to increase your advantage. Supply paper and pens for taking notes during the proceedings. Check the bathroom facilities, and make sure that the lighting in the negotiating room is adequate, especially if audio-visual aids are being used. Physical comfort can also be a decisive factor; lower the temperature of the negotiating room by a few degrees, or delay the refreshments, to encourage a quicker decision from your opponents. If proceedings extend over a break, serve refreshments away from the meeting table, and avoid alcoholic drinks.

33 Do not reveal all your tactics at once when negotiating.

◄ **PROVIDING REFRESHMENTS**
Although your team members may lose their appetites during protracted negotiations, they will not lose their thirst. The combination of tension, unfamiliar surroundings, and pressure makes throats dry, so always provide water.

34 If needed, ensure that all parties have access to private phone lines.

35 Take a laptop computer if you need to access company data.

TAKING CONTROL OF AN AWAY-GROUND NEGOTIATION

Some negotiators prefer to visit the opposition on their home territory. Use this ploy to imply a willingness to make an effort and give a positive start to the proceedings. One advantage you may gain by this approach is that you will be able to dictate the time of the meeting to exert maximum pressure on your hosts. If there is no fixed agenda in advance of the negotiation, upon arrival ask your hosts if they mind your setting one. The opposition may be willing to make this concession since you are on their home ground. If you do set the agenda in this way, you must take full advantage of the opportunity – ensure that you build into it the details that you want, and you will start to tip the scales in your favor.

USING SEATING PLANS

The way in which negotiators are seated around a table – whether facing each other in a confrontational manner or seated collaboratively at a round table – can have a marked effect on the tone and even the outcome of a negotiating session.

36 Make sure that the Leader can make eye contact with all the key players.

SEATING SMALL TEAMS

For negotiations between small teams, the parties often face each other across a rectangular table. This is the most formal and confrontational arrangement. To undermine the opposition, try to seat your team leader at the head of the table to create the impression that they control the proceedings.

To help soften any hardline attitudes that are hindering negotiations, make the seating as informal as possible, preferably using a round table.

▼ **SEATING YOUR TEAM**
For anything other than extremely formal negotiations, a team of five is the accepted maximum. The "across the table" approach, in which teams sit facing each other, is usual and is favored when negotiators want to emphasize their separate identities. Sit each member of the team where their skills will be of most use and in a way that presents a united front.

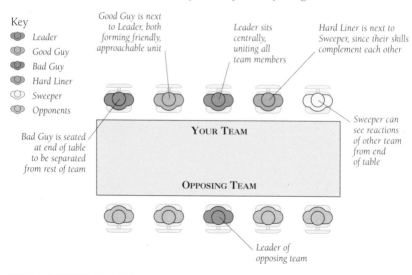

Key
- Leader
- Good Guy
- Bad Guy
- Hard Liner
- Sweeper
- Opponents

Good Guy is next to Leader, both forming friendly, approachable unit

Leader sits centrally, uniting all team members

Hard Liner is next to Sweeper, since their skills complement each other

Sweeper can see reactions of other team from end of table

YOUR TEAM

OPPOSING TEAM

Bad Guy is seated at end of table to be separated from rest of team

Leader of opposing team

USING SEATING TACTICALLY

When seating any size of team for negotiations, find the most comfortable chairs possible. As an alternative to the traditional or informal seating plan around a table, make it difficult for a visiting team to present a cohesive opposition by seating them among your own team. If possible, seat the most vocal or aggressive member of the visitors' team right next to the leader of your team.

However the teams are seated, eye contact is very important. It helps negotiators read the mood of the opposition and also enables team leaders to get feedback from their own team. The absence of eye contact is disorienting; you may wish to exploit this factor when seating your opponents.

37 Seat your Hard Liner away from your opponent's Hard Liner.

38 Position chairs at an equal distance from each other.

SEATING LARGE TEAMS

If negotiations are between many parties, with only a few representatives of each present (such as at the United Nations or the International Monetary Fund), seat the participants in a large circle, and arrange for individuals to speak from a podium to make their case.

If negotiations are between a few parties, each of which has a large number of representatives, divide the seating into groups, facing each other if possible. This is the way in which national parliaments are often seated and is an arrangement that can be used at either trade union or staff committee negotiations.

INFLUENCING SEATING PLANS

When you arrive at a negotiation hosted by others, ascertain whether there is a prearranged seating plan. If there is no plan, try to seat your team first at the negotiating table so that you can tactically select your positions. Your choice of seats will depend on the dynamics of your team – whether you want to present a united front by sitting together, prefer to divide your opponents by sitting among them, or want to take control at the head of the table.

If you have been allocated seats, try to determine whether there is any logic behind the arrangements. The plan may give clues about the other parties and their views, or your perceived status. Seating may suggest that the talks are expected to be informal, confrontational, or dominated by your hosts. Once you gauge the tone, you can alter your approach accordingly. If you are not happy with the seating arrangements, ask if they can be changed.

CONDUCTING A NEGOTIATION

Plan your opening negotiating moves carefully to establish a positive tone. Then stay alert and be flexible to create and make use of all your opportunities in the course of a negotiation.

JUDGING THE MOOD

Negotiating is as much about listening and observing as it is about talking. You need to be very alert to the mood of the negotiations, since this can change quickly. Being alert involves using all your senses to pick up signals given off by others.

39 Begin any negotiations with uncontroversial, general points.

40 Stress the need for agreement from the outset.

ANTICIPATING THE TONE

Your preparation should help you to anticipate how the opposition will approach the negotiation. Once in the negotiation, try to judge whether you anticipated correctly by noticing nonverbal signals, such as gestures. If you are expecting an aggressive start, try to confirm this by reading signals from the other team – if they appear tense, your suspicions may be correct.

▼ **STUDYING REACTIONS**
Throughout a negotiation, examine the other party's reactions and messages, trying to spot any inconsistencies.

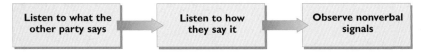

| Listen to what the other party says | Listen to how they say it | Observe nonverbal signals |

READING NONVERBAL SIGNALS

Nonverbal signals include body language, gestures, facial expressions, and eye movements. Learning to read body language among the opposition team will help you compile a true picture of their case – their signals may reinforce or contradict what they are saying. Clear-cut body language includes crossing of arms and legs, which betrays defensiveness, and leaning back on a chair, which expresses boredom. Small gestures and movements, such as hesitating or fidgeting, may indicate lack of conviction; raised eyebrows are a clear sign of surprise. Eye contact is another good source of information: team members may glance at each other when an important point in the negotiation has been reached.

41 Listen to a person's tone of voice as well as their words.

POINTS TO REMEMBER

- Speaking slowly and deliberately indicates that a person feels confident and at ease.
- Smiling unnecessarily and speaking quickly indicates nervousness.
- People who want to leave tend to look and turn their lower bodies toward the exit.

CULTURAL DIFFERENCES

Shaking hands may mean "Goodbye" to one party and "We've struck a deal" to the other. Make sure you understand the cultural rules before offering a handshake. In many Asian cultures, physical contact between the opposite sexes is discouraged. Women should therefore consider carefully whether to shake hands with men, or vice versa.

Direct eye contact is used

Handshake is firm but not overhearty

SETTING THE MOOD ▶
Shaking hands gives clues about the opposition. A confident handshake shows respect and openness; a forceful one indicates dominance; a limp one, passivity.

MAKING A PROPOSAL

Making a proposal is fundamental to all negotiation. It is vital to decide early on in the planning process whether you wish to speak first or to respond to the proposal from the opposition. This decision is a crucial part of negotiating strategy.

42 Put forward a proposal with as little emotion as possible.

KEEPING OPTIONS OPEN

43 Do not start speaking until you have something relevant to say.

Leave yourself plenty of room for maneuvering when presenting your case. Do not make brash statements that suggest that your position is immovable – make your proposals hypothetical to leave scope for both sides to make concessions at any time. Likewise, do not try to pin down the other party to a fixed position too soon – they need room to maneuver, too. Avoid forcing them into a corner or into making promises at an early stage of the proceedings, since this reduces their options when you come to make concessions later.

DO'S AND DON'TS

✔ Do listen carefully to the other party.

✔ Do leave enough room for maneuvering in your proposals.

✔ Do feel free to reject the first offer received.

✔ Do make conditional offers, such as "If you do this, we'll do that."

✔ Do probe the attitudes of the opposition: "What would be your feelings if…?"

✗ Don't make too many concessions at an early stage.

✗ Don't make your opening offer so extreme that you lose face if you need to back down.

✗ Don't ever say "never."

✗ Don't answer questions directly with a simple "yes" or "no."

✗ Don't make the opposition look foolish.

44 Pay close attention to the proposal of the other party.

45 Use humor when appropriate, but do not try to be too clever.

THINGS TO DO

1. Listen carefully to your opposition – their wishes may be closer to yours than you expect.

2. Be willing to adjust your strategy if you can see a compromise early on in the proceedings.

3. Make your initial offer unrealistic, and compromise from that point onward.

4. Take notes of all the offers made, trying to record them verbatim.

TIMING A PROPOSAL

The outcome of all negotiations depends on the presenting and discussing of proposals made by all parties concerned. These will be expanded and compromised upon until an agreement is reached. There are advantages in letting the other party make the opening proposal, since you may find that there is less distance between their demands and yours than you suspected. If this is the case, adjust your own strategy accordingly. If you decide to make the opening proposal, it will be generally regarded as unrealistic, so make your initial demands greater than you expect to receive, and offer less than you expect to give. If you open with an offer that you think is genuinely fair, there is a danger that the other party will interpret it as being very different from your actual requirements.

PHRASING A PROPOSAL

It is important that you present your initial proposal fluently and with confidence so you are taken seriously by your opponents. While speaking, emphasize the need to reach agreement, saying, for example: "I know that everybody here today is eager to see this project move forward as quickly as possible." When making your proposal, explain the conditions attached before making your initial offer. Summarize your offer briefly and then keep quiet to show that you have finished, allowing the other party time to digest your words.

Posture is open and confident

Direct eye contact is made with other party

MAKING A PROPOSAL ▶
Sit upright in your chair and lean forward slightly. Using positive body language such as this encourages the other party to take both you and your proposal seriously.

RESPONDING TO A PROPOSAL

Try to avoid showing any immediate reaction, favorable or otherwise, when responding to a proposal. Do not be afraid to remain silent while assessing the offer, but be aware that your opposition will be studying you to gauge your reaction.

46 Look for any similarities in your negotiating positions.

47 Wait for the other party to finish before responding.

SEEKING CLARIFICATION

When you have heard the other party's offer, do not feel obliged to respond immediately with a counteroffer. Remain as inscrutable as possible while summarizing the proposal as you have understood it. This gives you more time to think about what has been said and also provides an opportunity to confirm that you have understood it correctly. This is the time to focus on any issues that you feel unsure of and to challenge the other party to correct you. For example, "If I grasp what you are saying, we cannot expect to see any goods until next December," or "Can we clarify that you have taken into account the length of time it takes to clear checks in Singapore?" It is crucial that you understand the other party's position completely.

◀ **MAKING YOUR RESPONSE**
Use open body language – making eye contact, sitting upright with hands loosely crossed in front of you – to indicate that you have understood and accepted what has been offered to you. However, do not give away too much – keep the other party guessing about your reactions.

STALLING FOR TIME

Use stalling tactics only if you do not want to respond to your opponent's offer immediately, and then use them sparingly. These are the tactics that you can use without seriously jeopardizing the outcome of your negotiations:

- Interrupt the other party's proposal – but only if you can disguise this as seeking clarification of a point or refocusing the discussion;
- Answer a question with a question, or ask lots of questions – after all, it does no harm to have extra information at your disposal;
- Break off the negotiations for consultation with your colleagues, especially if you have already established that there is an external authority from whom you need to seek feedback.

48 Always use stalling tactics subtly and sparingly, if at all.

49 Indicate that every concession you make is a major loss to you.

50 Ask for a break to consider any new proposals.

PROPOSING ALTERNATIVES

If you decide to make a counteroffer, try to do so immediately after you have completed your assessment of the other team's offer – sometimes it is appropriate to strike while the iron is hot. To become a successful negotiator, learn to recognize that there are alternatives to every situation. Decide what you can offer as a counterproposal by working out which issues are priorities to your opposition. From these, identify the priorities that are least important to you, and incorporate them into your counteroffer. In this way you will appear willing to compromise but will not in fact give away anything of great value to your team.

In a classic example, two brothers are arguing about how to divide the last piece of pie. Each wants the larger slice. Their father suggests that one son cut the pie any way he wants and that the other then choose which piece he wants. Such a piece of lateral thinking can bring a negotiation to a speedy and satisfactory conclusion.

RESPONDING TO PLOYS

Good negotiators need to be able to recognize – and counter – the ploys and tactics that are commonly used by people during negotiation. Identify and resist manipulative tactics as they occur to avoid costly mistakes when negotiating.

51 If you are foiled by a successful ploy, think before you respond.

POINTS TO REMEMBER

- The unexpected introduction of new issues should be avoided.

- Ignoring a ploy will neutralize the intended effect.

- Personal attacks should be deflected with humor rather than allowed to provoke anger.

- Ploys used by the other team should not be taken personally. Be aware that they are used for manipulative purposes.

- Allocating blame for losing ground when the opposing team has employed a successful tactic is a waste of valuable time.

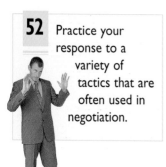

52 Practice your response to a variety of tactics that are often used in negotiation.

UNDERSTANDING PLOYS

It is common during negotiations to encounter tactics employed to enable one party to benefit while conceding as little as possible. These ploys work by creating the perception that your power to get what you want is inferior to that of the other party, thus lowering your resistance to giving the other party its own way.

While you may not choose to use these ploys, it is highly important for you to recognize and counter them so that you remain focused on your objectives and avoid wasting time on distractions.

IDENTIFYING PLOYS

Recognizing the tactics that other parties use to influence negotiations takes practice. To learn how to identify and deal with such ploys without risking expensive mistakes, observe the other parties very carefully and bear in mind that manipulative tactics usually have three main aims:

- To distract your team, allowing the opposition to dominate the discussions;
- To shift the emphasis of the negotiation in order to shape the deal on terms that are purely to the benefit of the opposition;
- To manipulate your team into closing negotiations before you are entirely satisfied with the terms being offered.

COUNTERING TYPICAL TACTICS

TACTICS	COUNTER-TACTICS
MAKING THREATS Warning of unwelcome repercussions if you fail to agree to the terms offered; emphasizing that penalties will be incurred by your side.	Tell the other party that you cannot negotiate under duress and that concessions will be made only if they can prove the merits of the case. Review other options available to you.
OFFERING INSULTS Questioning the performance of your company or your professional competence; criticizing the quality of your product or service.	Stay calm; do not lose your temper or offer insults in return. Restate your position firmly and warn that you will break off negotiations unless the other party is more constructive.
BLUFFING Threatening punitive action without being too specific; making dubious assertions, such as suggesting that competitors can undercut prices.	Call their bluff: refuse to agree to the other party's terms, then wait for a reaction. Question all statements and ask for evidence to support any claims that appear dubious.
USING INTIMIDATION Keeping you waiting; making you sit in an awkward or uncomfortable place; receiving phone calls or visitors during negotiations.	Recognize that these are ploys to make you feel less confident. Do not drop your original terms unless you have gained concessions in return, and do not be coerced into settling.
DIVIDING AND CONQUERING Exploiting potential disagreements among members of your team by appealing to the person most sympathetic to their case.	Brief team members in advance and decide on a position that is acceptable to everyone. Call an adjournment if differences of opinion arise within your team during the meeting.
USING LEADING QUESTIONS Asking you a series of questions that lead you to declare a weakness in your negotiating position; forcing concessions from your side.	Avoid answering questions when you do not understand the intention behind them. Check any claims made by the other party. Attach conditions to any concessions you make.
MAKING EMOTIONAL APPEALS Accusing you of acting unfairly in not agreeing to terms; stressing their sacrifices; claiming to be offended by your lack of trust.	Affirm your commitment to achieving a fair settlement on business terms. Ask questions to test the validity of manipulative claims. Lead the conversation back to discussing the issues.
TESTING THE BOUNDARIES Gaining additional concessions through minor infringements of the terms agreed, resulting in substantial gain over a long period.	Be clear on exactly what you are agreeing to when you reach a settlement. Draw up a clearly worded statement of terms agreed, and hold the other party to these at all times.

DEALING WITH UNHELPFUL BEHAVIOR

Emotional outbursts from attendees can suddenly change the mood of a negotiation. These outbursts may declare indecision, confusion, or aggression, but the most common type is a team member losing their temper. Unhelpful behavior works well as a ploy because it shifts attention from the issue under negotiation to one individual. When this occurs, decide whether it is a ploy or is unintentional, then steer the discussion back on course as quickly as possible. You cannot make a decision if you are not negotiating. Handle these situations well, and people will be less likely to try such ploys again.

53 Adjourn when an unknown element is introduced into a negotiation.

54 Engage only in arguments that are constructive.

HANDLING PLOYS AND UNHELPFUL BEHAVIOR

PROBLEMS	POSSIBLE SOLUTIONS
CONFUSED NEGOTIATOR	● Use visual aids to clarify complex issues that are causing confusion. ● Put complex proposals in writing, using short, clear sentences. ● Follow a concise step-by-step agenda to prevent further confusion. ● Be prepared to involve a third party to review the issues with a fresh eye.
INDECISIVE NEGOTIATOR	● Proceed slowly and methodically, and be prepared to reiterate points. ● Promise a review of the issues under discussion after a set period of time. ● Adjourn to allow an indecisive negotiator to consult others in their team. ● Try to present the issues in a fresh and original way.
AGGRESSIVE NEGOTIATOR	● Reiterate all the facts, keeping calm and avoiding emotional language. ● Refuse to be drawn into a battle of words, and stay calm at all times. ● State firmly that intimidation, bullying, and threats are unacceptable. ● Suggest an adjournment in the negotiations until tempers cool.
EMOTIONAL NEGOTIATOR	● Do not challenge the motives or integrity of the negotiator. ● Do not interrupt outbursts; wait patiently to make your response. ● Respond to any emotional outburst with rational questioning. ● Adjourn to allow the emotional negotiator to calm down.

ADJOURNING A NEGOTIATION

The natural way to cope with ploys such as emotional outbursts is through an adjournment. But an adjournment may itself be used as a stalling ploy, either by you or your opponent. If an adjournment is called for by one party, the other side must either accept or call off the negotiations.

Adjourn negotiations to allow the opposition to calm down and realize that losing their temper is unlikely to help them achieve their objectives. Alternatively, use an adjournment to review your position and tactics if new issues are introduced unexpectedly. However, be aware that adjournments can delay an agreement and become a disadvantage. If you call for an adjournment, summarize and record the discussion's progress before breaking.

55 Call for an adjournment when a completely new issue is introduced.

56 When you agree to talk off the record, always keep your word.

ADJOURNING FOR INFORMAL DISCUSSION

If formal negotiations have reached a stalemate, it may be helpful to continue the discussion on a different footing. Suggest that you talk off the record, without recording your conversation as part of the official minutes of the meeting and without either party being held to anything discussed. Encourage the other party to talk informally and in confidence about their reservations over making concessions. Move to another room nearby, if one is available, since a different environment may be more conducive to relaxed discussion. If experts disagree on a specific technical matter, suggest that they ask another expert for an independent opinion.

CHATTING IN CONFIDENCE ▶
An informal chat away from the formal table across which parties usually face each other can smooth out negotiations. Use such an opportunity to show an opponent that you are reasonable and approachable.

UNDERSTANDING BODY LANGUAGE

A lot can be learned about the attitude of the other side in a negotiation from their body language. Watch the eyes, which are the most expressive part of the body, but also pay attention to the rest of the face and the postures of members of the other team.

57 Assign one of your team to detect signals given off by the opposition.

READING BASIC SIGNS

Eye contact with another person indicates a desire to transmit and receive information. When talking, most people make eye contact with each other that lasts for a few seconds at regular intervals. Recognize that eye contact is one of the most important aspects of body language, but also take into account what your opponents are thinking by "reading" the signs given off by their gestures and their overall postures.

UNDERSTANDING SIGNS ▶
You need only a few seconds to obtain significant feedback about your opponents' initial reactions to what you are saying. Recognize and understand their expressions, and use this knowledge to your advantage. Pinpoint their most receptive listeners, then address your remarks to them.

58 Be alert. Key signals may last for only a second.

Open expression shows interest in proceedings

Leaning back implies hostility

Posture suggests attentiveness

Crossed arms indicate disbelief

EXPRESSING OPPOSITION

SHOWING INTEREST

DEALING WITH DUPLICITY

Skilled negotiators can use body language to mislead the other party in a debate. Do not take all body language at face value – it is easy to add a smile to an expression that is otherwise hostile. A person who fulfills the criteria for showing interest may in fact be preparing for a scathing attack. Therefore, always look at an individual's body language in conjunction with that of the members of the other party to get an average reading of the group's mood. It is essential to stay alert, even if you think that the negotiations are proceeding smoothly.

59 Learn to trust your instincts about other people's body language.

Wide eyes and warm expression indicate willingness to be persuaded

Direct eye contact implies positive thoughts

Inattentive gaze means lack of concentration

Open arms imply indecision

Hand on chin shows thoughtfulness

Fiddling with a pen confirms thoughts are elsewhere

MAKING DECISIONS

LACKING INTEREST

REMAINING NEUTRAL

ESTABLISHING POSITIONS

The negotiating process can begin in earnest once each team has explored their own position after hearing the other side's proposal. Start to move toward a mutually acceptable agreement once both parties have reassessed their positions.

60 Ask a lot of "how" questions to imply a willingness to compromise.

61 Watch for changes in body language, then adjust your tactics accordingly.

REINFORCING POSITIONS

After you have heard the other team's proposal, your team may need to reassess its strategy or tactics in order to retain a strong bargaining position. Look for any mutual points of interest between the two sides, and consider the points on which you are prepared to give or concede. Decide whether there are any major differences between the two cases that will require you to prepare a counterproposal in response to the opposition's proposal, or whether you need to make a few minor adjustments to reinforce your current position before beginning the debating stage.

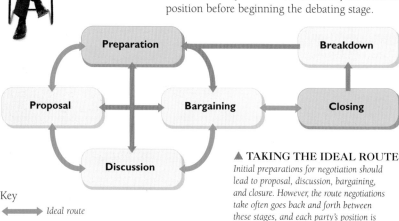

▲ TAKING THE IDEAL ROUTE

Initial preparations for negotiation should lead to proposal, discussion, bargaining, and closure. However, the route negotiations take often goes back and forth between these stages, and each party's position is likely to change with each revised proposal.

Key
→ Ideal route
← Other routes

READING FACIAL EXPRESSIONS

Most people involuntarily show their emotions in their facial expressions, so watch carefully for a triumphant twitch of the lips or a suppressed yawn. Such signals are particularly valuable at the debating stage, when parties are exploring their positions.

Tense jaw

Wide eyes

Steely gaze

Head tilted to side

Averted gaze

Hand touches ear

▲ **EXASPERATION**
The wide-eyed expression and raised eyebrows convey irritation tinged with frustration. Often, exasperation is experienced when progress is slow.

▲ **BOREDOM**
The tilted head, raised eyebrows, averted gaze, and set mouth all convey boredom. Use a lack of interest to your advantage to move the proceedings forward.

▲ **DISBELIEF**
The unconscious touching of the ear and evasive eye movements suggest that the listener is not convinced by what the other party is telling her.

POINTS TO REMEMBER

● Once you have established your position, use tactics to maintain it.

● Proposals should be revised to accommodate new information from the other party's proposal.

● All possible routes should be explored: "But if we were to do that, then would you…?"

● Always aim for a mutually beneficial outcome.

62 Summarize the assessment of your positions regularly.

DEBATING THE ISSUES

Once both parties have outlined their basic positions, there may be extensive discussion about the underlying assumptions and facts. This debating time is a crucial stage in the negotiating procedure. Use it to search for some common ground and strengthen your case.

Debate can easily become emotional and heated if accusations and counteraccusations are made. Keep every debate calm. If you are frustrated or angry, try not to let it show. Do not score points off the opposition; instead, work to form a bond with them. If they make a mistake, be aware that it strengthens your case, but allow them to retreat without loss of credibility. It may help if you start the discussion on points of mutual agreement before moving on to issues on which you disagree.

STRENGTHENING YOUR POSITION

Gaining the upper hand in negotiations reinforces an argument immediately. Introduce as many relevant points as possible to strengthen your position so that the opposing party is overwhelmed by the strength and thoroughness of your case.

63 Use repetition and positive body language to stress your key points.

KEEPING THE ADVANTAGE

Strength is about power – the power that you can wield to influence the outcome of a negotiation. When you have made a powerful point, maintain a strong position by reminding the other party of all the disadvantages of rejecting your proposal. Try to make it as easy as possible for the other side to change their position. This will help to strengthen relationships and avoid deadlock.

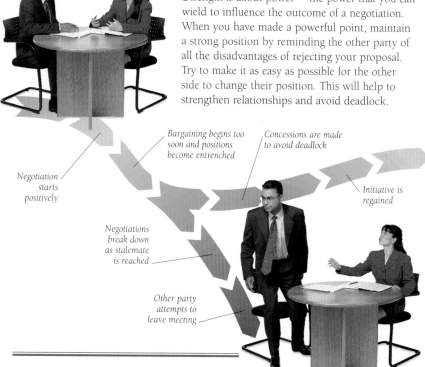

Bargaining begins too soon and positions become entrenched

Concessions are made to avoid deadlock

Negotiation starts positively

Initiative is regained

Negotiations break down as stalemate is reached

Other party attempts to leave meeting

64 Refer matters to a third party if you need an arbitrator to mediate.

65 Never undermine the dignity of the opposing party.

STAYING IN CONTROL

Negotiating can be a stressful process. Anxiety over the outcome may be heightened by worries about peer pressure and showing yourself in a favorable light. The negotiations may focus on an emotive issue, or you may feel threatened by the opposition's tactics. Never take things personally; otherwise, you may lose control of the situation. Concentrate on the issues and restate your position firmly if necessary. Avoid criticizing an antagonist, and never be tempted to resort to personal insults over the negotiating table.

If you are forced to make concessions to prevent negotiations from breaking down, attach your own conditions. This way, you will not need to give ground without receiving something in return.

Take the long-term view, and remember that compromise can be a constructive tactic to help you reach an agreement.

Agreement is reached

Final points of deal are discussed

▲ CLINCHING A DEAL

This illustration shows two of the possible routes a negotiation can take. Despite a very positive start, the proceedings can be followed by deterioration to the point of breakdown. In this scenario, the negotiators avoid deadlock in their meeting by making concessions and compromising on minor issues in order to reach a mutually satisfactory outcome.

POINTS TO REMEMBER

● Your points should be reiterated in a loud but calm voice – assertively but not aggressively.

● Emphasizing the positive hides the negative; for example, "We may not have made a profit last year, but look at this year's figures."

● Any mistakes should be acknowledged immediately so you can carry on with confidence.

● Appearing arrogant may hinder your chances of reaching an agreement with the other party.

● A deal is made, not won. Opponents should be persuaded that the deal will benefit everyone.

● Your original aims should be firmly fixed in your mind.

WEAKENING THE OTHER PARTY'S POSITION

To achieve a successful outcome in negotiations, strengthen your own position and look for ways to weaken the opposition at the same time. Use one or more of a range of tactics to diminish your opponent's influence in negotiations.

66 Press home your advantage when the opposition loses momentum.

UNDERMINING OPPONENTS

When negotiating, undermine the other party's confidence, and even their credibility, but only by casting doubt on the validity of their information. Continually test the validity of your opponent's case; look for weakness such as errors of logic, misuse of statistics, omissions of fact, and hidden agendas. Avoid the temptation to try to weaken the other party's position by attacking individual personalities. You may face a backlash if the opposition responds in similar vein. Unprovoked attacks are also unlikely to gain you sympathy with a third party if one is called in to mediate or arbitrate.

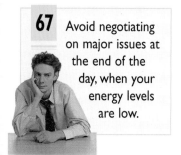

67 Avoid negotiating on major issues at the end of the day, when your energy levels are low.

USING EMOTION

A show of emotion at the negotiating table may convince others of your feelings and the honesty of your argument, helping weaken the other party's position. Use this tactic sparingly, however; repeated displays will be increasingly ineffectual. Emotional outbursts can also backfire unless handled carefully; instead of swaying the opposition, they may inflame tempers and lead to a breakdown in the negotiations.

68 Continually test for weaknesses in the other party's position.

Recognizing Errors

An effective way to weaken your opponent's position is to find errors of fact or logic in their proposals. Look out for the selective use of statistics: if you are presented with details that seem too good to be true, ask about the things that are not being talked about. They may be hiding the bad news. If you find flaws, bring them immediately to everybody's attention.

Points to Remember

- Threats may not weaken the opponent – and they may backfire.
- If one party contains employees on strike, they will enter into negotiations having already made an impact on their opposition.
- Teamwork can help maintain pressure on your opponents.

Using Tactics to Weaken the Opposition

Types of Tactic	Examples of How to Use Tactics
Financial Imposing costs on one or both parties if agreement is not reached.	- Inform the other parties that costs will be incurred if, for example, goods are held in a warehouse until it is possible to resolve a dispute over their ownership. - Point out to the opposition that opportunity costs will occur if the negotiation is prolonged.
Legal Using sanctions/injunctions to prevent one party from taking action or to cause delays to proceedings.	- Threaten to pursue a course of legal action, if you have a solid case, and emphasize the cost, both in time and money, to the other party if they lose. - Cause lengthy legal wrangles to effect delays in production and consequently loss of finance to achieve an agreement.
Social Imposing restrictions by disapproving of a proposed course of action on moral grounds.	- Tell your opponents that their proposals are an insult to the people they are likely to affect. - Demonstrate how unfair suggested proposals are when compared to the treatment that other people receive in similar situations.
Humiliation Publicly humiliating one party or individual in the eyes of their peers.	- Humiliate an opposing party in order to damage their image or reputation. This can cause some long-term damage to their credibility but is unlikely to have any drastic effect on the party's business. Be aware that they may seek revenge for the humiliation in the future.
Emotional Making opponents feel guilty if they do not make any concessions.	- Emotionally blackmail your opponent if they are not giving you enough ground. Note that this tactic can be uneven in its effectiveness. Sometimes, people who feel they have been emotionally manipulated may be even more unwilling to make concessions in the future.

CLOSING A NEGOTIATION

A negotiation can be brought to a successful conclusion only when both parties have made concessions that are mutually acceptable in order to reach an agreement.

TRADING POSITIONS

Trading positions is a delicate process of bargaining whereby each party makes concessions to reach an agreement. However, if you are the weaker party, or your main aim is to minimize your losses, bargaining can be stressful and costly.

69 Offer the smallest concessions first – you may not need to go any further.

70 Make steady eye contact to emphasize that each concession is a serious loss for you.

MAKING CONCESSIONS

When you are forced to make concessions, it is important that you take a long-term view. Try to retain some control of the situation by:

- Judging how much ground you need to yield – put a value on what you are prepared to give so that it can be matched with concessions from the other side;
- Compromising without losing face. For example, if you need to backtrack on a point you had established as your final position, you can say, "Since you have changed your position on…, we may be able to change ours on…"

MAKING HYPOTHETICAL PROPOSALS

Test how flexible your opponents may be by making hypothetical proposals before giving concessions. "If" is the important word in the questions below, which do not commit you to anything yet may help you to identify the issues important to the other party.

❝ If we come up with another million, will you give us the Rome operation and the cargo boat? ❞

❝ If I reduce the price by 20 percent, will you give me firm orders in advance? ❞

❝ If I give you 90 days credit instead of 60, will you give me the interest that you would have paid? ❞

DISCUSSING TERMS

As you near the end of a negotiation, you need to discuss the terms of your agreement. Use your hypothetical proposals to help you work out a basic deal. The terms of the deal will involve the method of payment, the schedule of payment, how long the agreement should stand before being revised, and what to do if any problems arise over implementation of the deal – whether, for example, arbitration should be sought.

71 Do not concede ground unless you receive something in return.

TRADING ▶ SUCCESSFULLY
Here is an example of a successful negotiation. The dealer establishes how much his customer wants to pay, and the customer gets what she wants at a price she can afford.

CASE STUDY

Jane wanted a red carpet she had seen in a store window. She walked into the store and asked how much it was. The dealer did not tell her but knew it cost him $150, and he offered Jane a cup of coffee. Jane began to get defensive and said she really wanted something with more brown in it. "I have lovely brown carpets," said the dealer, offering to show her some. Backtracking again, Jane said she wanted a denser pile, and again the dealer said that he had such a carpet.

So Jane decided to negotiate to get the red carpet. She asked the price again. He told her it was $700. "That is too much," said Jane, starting to walk away. She offered $300. "You can have it for $650," said the dealer. "No, thank you," Jane said, walking toward the door. Believing he would lose a sale, the dealer let Jane buy it for $300, doubling his outlay. Both were happy with the deal.

NEGOTIATING A PACKAGE

As you move toward closing a negotiation and start to discuss terms, try to draw together the various items under negotiation. Group related items together, rather than negotiating for each individually. This gives you scope to make painless concessions: you can yield ground on issues of lesser importance within the package to gain extra leverage for your main objective. For example, do not concentrate only on a new pay deal. Link pay with demands for longer vacations, higher pension contributions, and more generous health benefits. Be prepared to concede on pension and vacation demands to gain your main objective of shorter working hours. Negotiating a package is also a good way of finding out the true priorities of the opposition. Thus, you may be dealing with another party that needs to fill a half-empty cargo ship and so is not too concerned about the price per item of the consignment of goods.

72 Make concessions on a minor issue to lessen intransigence on a major one.

73 Remind the other party of areas of agreement to help break a deadlock.

CONCENTRATING ON ▶ ELEMENTS OF A PACKAGE

This pie chart shows an example of the proportions of time spent in a negotiation between employers and staff on various aspects of a pay and benefits package. The most time was spent on salaries – the top priority for the staff. They were prepared to concede to their employer's demands about vacations and pensions to spend more time on their principal aim.

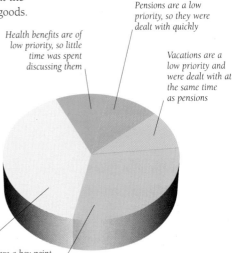

Pensions are a low priority, so they were dealt with quickly

Health benefits are of low priority, so little time was spent discussing them

Vacations are a low priority and were dealt with at the same time as pensions

Key

■ *Health benefits*

■ *Pensions*

Vacations

Working hours

Salaries

Salaries are the major priority, so they took up most of the discussion

Working hours are a key point for the employees, so they took up considerable negotiation time

AVOIDING REJECTION

The benefit of packaging proposals together is that the least important elements can be rejected without either party losing face, while using hypothetical proposals enables you to refine your negotiations until a compromise is reached. In both cases, you can gain valuable insight into what your opposition is prepared to accept – as well as what they might relinquish – based on their reactions to your bargaining.

Avoid situations in which your final offer will be rejected. This undermines your negotiating position and may make it hard to restore a favorable balance of power in the negotiations. For example, if the other party says, "Your final offer of $400 is totally unacceptable," a response of "What if we raise it to $500?" signals a serious loss of credibility on your part. Prevent outright rejection by refining your package as you edge closer to an agreement.

RECORDING A DEAL

Once you have successfully completed your negotiations, summarize your agreement in writing and obtain everyone's approval of the summary. This avoids confusion and possible hostility later on. Remember that the summary must clearly record who gets what, how, and when, and the action to be taken. Both parties must sign the agreement. Clarify any ambiguous terminology, such as "adequate," "fair," or "significant," at this stage. If there is not enough time to obtain everybody's written agreement immediately, record the conclusion of the negotiations (either on an electronic notepad, a tape recorder, or in note form), and have a detailed set of minutes drawn up immediately after the meeting. Send a copy to the other party, and ask for their written confirmation that the minutes represent a true and fair view of the result of the negotiations. Speed in circulating the minutes is essential, because if there is confusion or disagreement over what has been agreed you can reopen negotiations and resolve the problem quickly.

MAKING ▶ RECORDS
Take notes or use electronic organizers to record agreements during a negotiation.

CHOOSING HOW TO CLOSE

As you draw near to completing an agreement, check that all parties share the same understanding of the issues, then confirm what has been agreed and close the negotiation. There are various ways of closing, so select the one that suits your team.

74 Record fully all agreements finalized at a negotiation's close.

FOCUSING ON ISSUES

Before moving toward closure of a negotiation, it is important to ensure you are clearly focused on the relevant issues and that you have not allowed personal feelings about the other side's negotiating tactics to color your judgment and decisions. Are you holding out for a higher price because you need to make a profit, or just so the other party does not feel they have beaten you down?

75 Read over any notes covering the early part of your negotiations.

CONFIRMING TERMS

At this stage in a negotiation, it is important to be sure that all parties are talking about the same thing. Examine the terminology you are intending to use in your final agreement. If you are drawing up a commercial contract, define any key terms or use easily understood vocabulary. It is vital that your terms are recorded clearly and accurately, since both parties agree to abide by these conditions in the event of a dispute. Reviewing both teams' understanding of the agreement in this way can also highlight previously unnoticed misunderstandings. The close of the negotiations must include ironing out these problems, which may give you or the other party room to negotiate new concessions. For example: "If I'd realized that you meant delivery in New York, I would never have agreed to such high freight costs – let's look at it again."

76 Discuss and define any words that might be ambiguous in a written format.

77 Make sure you do not ignore issues in order to speed up negotiations.

METHODS OF CLOSING A NEGOTIATION

METHODS OF CLOSURE	FACTORS TO CONSIDER
MAKING CONCESSIONS THAT ARE ACCEPTABLE TO ALL PARTIES Proposing and accepting concessions that help clinch the deal without jeopardizing your party's position.	● This continuation of the process of trading can break a deadlock. ● The other party may be tempted to try gaining even more concessions. ● Making concessions late in the negotiations may undermine your credibility.
SPLITTING THE DIFFERENCE BETWEEN ALL PARTIES Agreeing between all sides involved in the negotiations to move toward the middle ground in order to reach a deal.	● It may be difficult to judge what is a fair split of the difference. ● This is an indication that you are still prepared to make some concessions. ● Neither party will feel that they have won or lost at the end of the negotiations.
GIVING ONE PARTY A CHOICE OF TWO ACCEPTABLE ALTERNATIVES Encouraging the other party to move forward by offering them two different options from which to choose.	● This suggests that any "final" offer you have already made was not really your last call. ● Finding two options that are equally acceptable to you may not be easy. ● There is no guarantee that the other party will agree to either of the proposals.
INTRODUCING NEW INCENTIVES OR SANCTIONS Bringing pressure to bear on the other party by introducing new incentives or sanctions.	● The threat of sanctions may increase the opposition's feelings that you are being hostile. ● Introducing new incentives can completely alter the balance of a negotiation. ● This can provide the push necessary to bring the other party to agreement.
INTRODUCING NEW IDEAS OR FACTS AT A LATE STAGE Bringing new ideas to the meeting table provides an incentive for new discussion and may lead to an agreement.	● This gives the other party room to see new concessions that they could make. ● This may undermine your credibility – you should have introduced the new ideas earlier. ● This may undermine the basis of the negotiation and take you back to square one.
SUGGESTING AN ADJOURNMENT WHEN STALEMATE OCCURS Adjourning allows each side in the negotiations time to consider what will happen if there is no agreement.	● This gives each party an opportunity to consult with outside advisers. ● Circumstances may change the position of the parties during the adjournment. ● It may prove to be too difficult to reconvene a further meeting at another time.

MOVING TO A CLOSE

Having chosen your method of closing, you can now move to execute it – but be aware of any shifts of mood in the other party. Timing your final offer to coincide with an upbeat phase in the talks can make the difference between success and failure.

78 Be assertive but not aggressive when you are closing a deal.

TIMING YOUR OFFER

An offer presented at the wrong moment may be rejected, while exactly the same offer – presented at a different moment – is accepted. Make your final offer when the other party is receptive, using all your skills to produce the right atmosphere:

- Praise the other party – "That was an excellent point. I think that in view of that I can offer…"
- Be self-deprecating – "I'm afraid that I've been unable to come up with any bright ideas, but I think we could agree to…"
- Emphasize how far you have come together – "I think we've made really good progress today, and I feel able to offer…"

79 Make sure your opponent has full authority to close the deal.

▼ CLOSING A DEAL
When a team of negotiators is about to make a closing move, they will look to their leader to take the first step.

Team leader summarizes and makes final offer

Body language is supportive

Team member backs up leader with data

LEADING UP TO AN OFFER

As you near conclusion, beware of "crying wolf." Earlier in the process, you may have felt a need to imply that certain offers were "final." This tactic is often used, but be careful not to say in so many words that a proposal is final when you know it is not, since this may prevent the other party from believing your "final final offer." Think in advance how to indicate this final final offer. Make it clear that you would prefer not to strike any deal than to compromise any further on the proposed terms.

80 Look at the other party when making your final offer.

81 If you are not satisfied with a deal, do not sign it.

MAKING A FINAL OFFER

Indicate to the other party that you are making your final final offer by choosing the right words, tone of voice, and body language. Create an atmosphere of decisiveness: gather up your papers, stand up, walk about, and generally look as if you intend to leave (in contrast to previous offers, when you may have been leisurely leaning back in your chair, implying that you expected the negotiations to continue). Increase the urgency and firmness of your tone of voice, but do not rush to close the negotiations.

REINFORCING A FINAL OFFER

A carefully selected phrase can indicate that you are about to make your final offer. Use firm, unequivocal language when making your final offer, and reinforce the impact of your words by using a calm, authoritative tone of voice and maintaining steady eye contact.

❝ I have no authority from our head office to make another offer. ❞

❝ This is my final final offer. I have no room whatsoever to move further than this. ❞

❝ I have already gone much further than I intended to go. ❞

❝ I am running out of time. Agree to my proposal, or I will need to leave for another meeting. ❞

ENCOURAGING CLOSURE

When you have made your final offer, the other party may simply accept it as it stands. If they do not, you may be able to nudge them toward making a final offer acceptable to you. Look for points that have not occurred to them – even apparently trivial ones – that could help you reach an agreement. Try to put yourself in the other party's shoes and to understand what might be preventing them reaching an agreement.

82 Emphasize the common ground you have found during a debate.

HELPING THE OTHER PARTY TO MOVE TO A CLOSE

METHODS	RESULTS
EMPHASIZING BENEFITS Concentrate on explaining to the other party how the proposed deal will be of benefit to them. However, you should avoid mentioning how the same deal will benefit your own side.	● Helps the other party to see advantages in agreeing to a deal that they may not previously have considered. ● Creates the perception of a win/win situation rather than a win/lose situation.
ENCOURAGING AND APPLAUDING Welcome any constructive proposal by the other party, no matter how long it takes to emerge. If you do not want to agree to it, you can still reject it later on in the negotiations.	● Creates a positive mood in which to move negotiations toward a close. ● Allows you to avoid critisism of your own counterproposals. ● Avoids antagonizing the other party at what may be a critical point in the debate.
AVOIDING A WIN/LOSE SITUATION Point out that you are looking for an outcome that is equally acceptable to both parties. Do not push through an acceptance that your opponents will later feel has been forced upon them.	● Avoids confrontation, which is likely to result in increasing hostility and deadlock. ● Fosters a relaxed atmosphere in which constructive discussion can take place. ● Allows counterproposals to be made.
SAVING FACE Give the other party an escape route by asking hypothetical questions or making hypothetical proposals, such as "How would you feel about...?" or "What if we...?"	● Increases the likelihood of your proposals being given proper consideration by the other party. ● Means the other party feels under less pressure to accept or reject your proposals, but may come to a decision sooner.

WORKING TOWARD COMPROMISE

At every stage of a negotiation, try to create a culture of compromise. By the time you are near closing, the other party should know that you are flexible and are not dogmatic about any issues. If the debate has followed a proper course, an atmosphere of compromise should have developed naturally. Each party will have realized that the other's argument has points in its favor and that each side must compromise at certain points. Even toward the end of the process, try to hold on to a few bargaining chips (minor issues that can be conceded easily) to trade if necessary. Do not respond too hastily to the other party's offers. They may continue to suggest new approaches that you had not considered before.

83 Try to understand the other party's hesitancy.

84 Agree on a date to review concessions made to break a deadlock.

POINTS TO REMEMBER

- A little ambiguity may enhance a proposal. There is an old saying: "The wheels of diplomacy turn on the grease of ambiguity."

- A sudden leap forward can make the opposition nervous. It is best to move slowly.

- There is a saying: "It is better to sell the wool than the sheep." Main objectives should not be conceded, but small points can be.

- Phrases that seem to lay down the law, such as "I insist on...," should be avoided.

85 Be polite but persistent. This will gain you respect.

OVERCOMING LAST-MINUTE HESITATION

There is always extra sensitivity on both sides of a negotiating table when a deal looks near to conclusion. The time between reaching a verbal agreement and signing on the dotted line is particularly delicate. Negotiators often get nervous and may try to back out at this stage.

If the other party is hesitant, sympathize with them. Remind them that the deal means changes for you, too, and that you are also nervous about it. If the other party persists in trying to back out, point out to them that this dishonorable behavior will tarnish their reputation, leaving them with an image of unreliability that may affect future negotiations. If you are in a position that allows you to force the deal through despite the objections of the opposition, remember this may well affect future negotiations with the same party.

HANDLING BREAKDOWN

When negotiations break down, immediate action is vital to prevent the situation becoming irretrievable. The longer an acrimonious breakdown is left to fester, the more bitter it becomes and the harder it is to restore a balanced attitude.

86 Avoid the temptation to respond with "an eye for an eye."

▼ LEAVING IN ANGER

Breakdowns often occur when one party stands up in anger and leaves the meeting. If this happens, the other negotiators need to think carefully about how to restore the discussion.

LIMITING DAMAGE

To limit the damage from a breakdown in negotiations, the two parties should reestablish communication as quickly as possible. The best way to do this is in a face-to-face meeting. However, if a breakdown has been very acrimonious, it may be more appropriate to make overtures of reconciliation in writing. E-mails are perfect for this because they are private and fast.

Angry negotiator unwilling to continue discussion

Team member explaining colleague's action

Opposition leader responds angrily to walkout

Opposition team member rises to retrieve situation

HEALING A RIFT

Try to retrieve a breakdown without appealing to outside help. If one member of a team has walked out of a meeting, persuade their colleagues to bring them back. If an entire team leaves, send the individual on your team who has the strongest relationship with them (possibly the Good Guy) to bring them back immediately. Do not allow a breakdown to continue if the consequence of no deal is worse than the last deal that was on the table. If a breakdown cannot be remedied internally, then you may need to call a third party, such as a conciliator, a mediator, or an arbitrator.

> **87** Do not insist on an apology when order has been restored.

◀ ORCHESTRATING A BREAKDOWN

Since one of Joe's objectives was to protect his supply line with Kim's company, walking out was a poor way to deal with a frustrating situation. The future relationship was undermined by Joe's outburst. It would have been better to bring in a third party to mediate.

CASE STUDY

Joe went to Taiwan to reclaim money from Kim's company for a shipment of bicycles that Joe's employer claimed were faulty. Joe knew there were other suppliers happy to provide him with bikes, but he was unwilling to disturb Kim's well-established supply line. Kim had no power to financially compensate Joe; she could only replace the bikes. Joe said that would not be enough to restore his company's reputation with purchasers of faulty goods.

Joe was booked on a plane leaving in three hours and saw nothing to be gained from listening politely to Kim's stonewalling. He stood up angrily and left the room. Kim was embarrassed but did not want to lose face by asking him to return.

Joe now buys his bikes in the US, and Kim's company has suffered as a result.

> **88** Contact the other party immediately after a walkout.

> **89** Agree a date for future talks to limit damage.

HANDLING INTENTIONAL BREAKDOWNS

There are occasions when one party actively wants negotiations to break down. If your team comes up with an unexpected bit of information that completely undermines the opposition's case, they may choose to give in on the spot, ask for an adjournment, or manipulate a breakdown in the negotiation. While this is not helpful, they may feel strongly that continuing will be harmful to their case. If this occurs, stay calm and try to amend the situation by effecting a reconciliation.

USING A MEDIATOR

When you have explored all the avenues, and the parties involved in a negotiation have still not reached an agreement, a mediator may be necessary. By agreeing to use a mediator, all parties are expressing a desire to resolve the situation.

90 View the use of a third party as a positive step, not a failing.

91 Think twice before using mediation – it is expensive.

ROLE OF A MEDIATOR ▼
The ideal mediator is unbiased, considers all angles, is acceptable to both parties, understands the issues, helps parties to find their own solutions, and prepares recommendations quickly.

UNDERSTANDING THE PROCESS OF MEDIATION

Mediation is the process in which deadlocked parties consider the suggestions of a third party, agreed upon in advance, but are not bound to accept the mediator's recommendations. The mediator acts as a referee between the negotiating parties and tries to find common ground among their agendas. Once some common ground is established, the mediator can begin to find mutually acceptable routes out of the deadlock.

Helps opposing parties understand each other

Helps parties create their own solutions

Considers problem from all angles

Suggests other solutions

Is impartial at all times

Explains issues to each side

CHOOSING A MEDIATOR

A mediator must be acknowledged by both parties as unbiased and must also be sufficiently knowledgable and informed about the points at issue to be able to make sensible recommendations that are relevant to both parties.

It is tempting to appoint a person in a position of authority (a former senior employee with experience in the field or a retired diplomat, for example) as a mediator. Although their authority may influence the final outcome, a mediator's capacity to adjudicate effectively is limited if they do not have the ability to recommend a solution. Consider using a less obvious person to mediate: someone, for example, who can think laterally, who has no preconceptions about the deadlock, and who can come up with a variety of creative suggestions for the best solutions to a stalemate.

92 Ensure mediators act while the parties are still eager to proceed.

93 Consider unconventional suggestions to resolve a deadlock.

DEVELOPING THE ROLE OF NEGOTIATOR-AS-MEDIATOR

You can help the smooth running of a negotiation by adopting a dual role from the very beginning. In the first role, you are a negotiator with specific objectives; in the second role, you are a mediator attempting to reconcile your objectives with those of the other party. In short, try to achieve your own objectives while finding common ground and presenting recommendations that are mutually acceptable to both parties.

It is essential to match a versatile and diplomatic personality to the role of negotiator-as-mediator. Ask yourself if you have a personality that is naturally suited to this dual role: do you look for balance in your life, and do you tend to make "we" statements as opposed to "I" statements? Avoid using forceful or aggressive members of your team in this role – they may be better at holding the floor and making proposals but will need to stand aside if negotiations break down.

▶ BALANCING ROLES
The role of negotiator-as-mediator requires you to be unbiased to ensure that the best interests of both parties are met.

GOING TO ARBITRATION

If a negotiation breaks down, you can resolve the dispute by using arbitration. This involves introducing a third party to help break the deadlock. Under the rules of arbitration, both sides are required to abide by the final decision given by the arbitrator.

94 It is worth paying as much as you can afford for good arbitration.

95 Ensure that you fully understand the process of arbitration.

CHOOSING ARBITRATION

If you need to go to arbitration, there are several options open to you. Use your industry's semi-permanent arbitration bodies or procedures for settling disputes, if it has them. Alternatively, ask an independent tribunal, individual, or professional body to arbitrate for you. However, since this requires the involvement of qualified experts and the establishment of formal agreements, such arbitration is slow and expensive – so make sure that there are no other options available to you.

AN ARBITRATOR'S ROLE ▼
The ideal arbitrator is unbiased, respected by all parties, empowered to enforce judgments, and discreet about findings.

Helps both parties reach their solutions

Adjudicates between both parties

Remains impartial during negotiations

Considers problems that cause deadlock

Is knowledgable about all issues

Reaches decisions enforceable by law

THE ADVANTAGES OF USING AN ARBITRATOR

The arbitrator's role in proceedings is to decide on a fair agreement between the negotiating parties, and then to enforce this ruling. Arbitration effectively bars negotiators from leaving the table without an agreement, although in extreme cases the courts can be asked to implement a decision.

Collect all the information available from both sides in the dispute to enable the arbitrator to assess your case in detail. You will benefit from this process since the arbitration service works independently – the case for each party is heard in confidence, and the final decision is released only to the parties concerned. This is particularly important in commercial disputes – many firms will go to great lengths to avoid the publicity that accompanies the majority of court judgments.

96 Choose an arbitrator that both sides can trust completely.

97 If necessary, ask a third party to appoint an arbitrator for you.

USING THE COURTS TO IMPLEMENT DECISIONS

The courts are a last resort for negotiating teams – after they have failed to reach agreement among themselves and if the judgments of independent third parties are not acceptable through either mediation or arbitration. Any legal process is likely to be expensive and to bring the dispute into the public arena. This often exposes negotiators to new and undesirable pressures, so always take legal advice before instituting judicial proceedings. For example, a company with a short-term cash-flow problem should try to reach private rescheduling agreements with its creditors. If these problems end up in court, it is in grave danger of being declared bankrupt, in which case both the company and its creditors could come out with nothing.

IMPLEMENTING DECISIONS

Once you have reached an agreement, either independently or with the help of a third party, your final decisions need to be implemented. Draw up a plan of action, then appoint appropriate members of your organization to put this plan into effect.

98 Agree an order in which the action agreed on should be fulfilled.

99 Draw up a final schedule for implementing the action agreed on.

AGREEING ON ACTION

Whenever agreement is reached between parties in a negotiation, the terms should be recorded and signed as an indication of multilateral approval and acceptance. Next, you must agree on how to implement the decisions. You may feel that it is appropriate to appoint a joint team to put the plans into action, or, alternatively, you may prefer to ask an independent party to oversee the project. Decide early on in the planning stage whether you wish for sanctions to be applied if the agreed action is not carried out to your deadlines – such measures can take the form of legal action or financial penalties. Unexpected problems will often arise at the implementation stage of an agreement, so appoint a team leader to monitor the process rigorously.

CASE STUDY

Stefan ran a small design firm and won the contract to refurbish a large office building. He negotiated an agreement on the timing and cost of the work and set a completion deadline of six months.
Knowing that he could not complete the work by himself, Stefan then hired an interior designer to procure the soft furnishings for the building, and an administration assistant to oversee the daily running of the project. This freed him to concentrate on restructuring the building itself.
As the work progressed, it became apparent that Stefan did not have time to deal with the teams of plumbers and electricians working in the building. He handed over this responsibility to his assistant, briefing her very carefully and issuing a schedule of tight deadlines for her to adhere to. The work was completed early and within budget.

◀ **UTILIZING A TEAM WELL**
Once he had negotiated his agreement, Stefan made the best use of the talents of his team by allocating them specific responsibilities. When he rethought his tactics, he briefed his assistant thoroughly and gave her a strict deadline to complete the work on time.

ASSIGNING A TEAM

The people assigned to implement any negotiated agreement may not have taken part in the actual discussions. For them, the provision of clear and accurate information is vital. When appointing a team and allocating specific tasks, pay special attention to the brief. Who is best suited to each task, and who needs to know what? How will team members receive information, and from whom? When will they receive updates, and how long will they be given to act on the information?

> **100** Decide who needs regular updates on the progress of your agreement.

> **101** Make a good last impression. It can be as important as the first one.

SCHEDULING IMPLEMENTATION

A negotiated decision is not considered a success until it has been enforced, so build deadlines and a plan of action into any agreements made around the negotiating table. Check the progress of your plan of action frequently – any slippage in the schedule may affect the agreed package, especially if major concessions were granted on the basis of meeting set targets. If other problems arise, resolve them by holding further negotiations.

◀ **REACTING POSITIVELY**
Engender good will around a negotiating table by reacting positively and enthusiastically when reaching a final agreement on how to implement decisions. Smile, shake hands, and congratulate each other warmly.

ASSESSING YOUR ABILITY

Everyone is *frequently involved in negotiation at work and at home, but in order to be truly successful at it you need to assess your skills. Evaluate your performance by responding to the following statements, then mark the options that are closest to your experience. Be as honest as you can: if your answer is "never," mark Option 1; if it is "always," mark Option 4; and so on. Add your scores together, then refer to the Analysis to see how you scored. Use your answers to identify which areas need improving.*

OPTIONS
1 Never
2 Occasionally
3 Frequently
4 Always

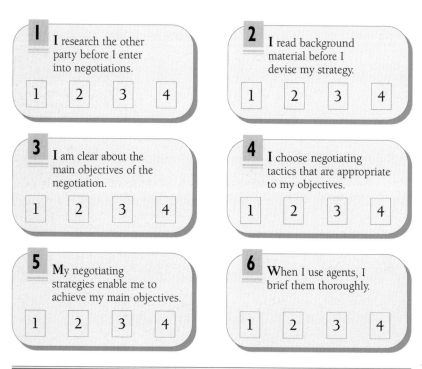

1 I research the other party before I enter into negotiations.

1   2   3   4

2 I read background material before I devise my strategy.

1   2   3   4

3 I am clear about the main objectives of the negotiation.

1   2   3   4

4 I choose negotiating tactics that are appropriate to my objectives.

1   2   3   4

5 My negotiating strategies enable me to achieve my main objectives.

1   2   3   4

6 When I use agents, I brief them thoroughly.

1   2   3   4

7 When I use agents, I aim to give them as much authority as they need.

1   2   3   4

8 I have a flexible attitude toward negotiations.

1   2   3   4

9 I believe negotiations to be an opportunity for both parties to benefit.

1   2   3   4

10 I enter into negotiations determined to reach a satisfactory agreement.

1   2   3   4

11 I communicate my points in plain language.

1   2   3   4

12 I communicate my points logically and clearly.

1   2   3   4

13 I consciously use body language to communicate with the other party.

1   2   3   4

14 I avoid exposing the other party's weaknesses.

1   2   3   4

15 I am polite at all times during the negotiation.

1   2   3   4

16 I create deadlines that are realistic and determined by the negotiation.

1   2   3   4

17 I use my instincts to help me understand the other party's tactics.

1 2 3 4

18 I have enough power to make decisions when necessary.

1 2 3 4

19 I am sensitive to any cultural differences of the other party.

1 2 3 4

20 I work well as a member of a negotiating team.

1 2 3 4

21 I am able to be objective and put myself in the position of the other party.

1 2 3 4

22 I know how to guide the other party into making an offer.

1 2 3 4

23 I avoid making the opening offer.

1 2 3 4

24 I make progress toward agreement via a series of conditional offers.

1 2 3 4

25 I approach my final objectives step by step.

1 2 3 4

26 I show emotion only as part of a tactical move.

1 2 3 4

27 I regularly summarize the progress that has been made during negotiations.

1   2   3   4

28 I use adjournments tactically to give me time to think.

1   2   3   4

29 I introduce third parties when the negotiations break down.

1   2   3   4

30 I employ a mediator as an effective way of breaking a stalemate.

1   2   3   4

31 I ensure that any agreement is signed by each party.

1   2   3   4

32 I prefer to negotiate a win/win situation whenever possible.

1   2   3   4

ANALYSIS

Now that you have completed the self-assessment, add up your total score and check your performance by reading the corresponding evaluation. Whatever level of success you have achieved when negotiating, it is important to remember that there is always room for improvement. Identify your weakest areas, then refer to the sections in this book where you will find practical advice and tips to help you establish and hone your negotiating skills.

32–64: Your negotiating skills are weak. Learn to use and recognize the strategies and tactics essential to successful negotiation.
65–95: You have reasonable negotiating skills, but certain areas need further improvement.
96–128: Your negotiations are successful. Continue to prepare thoroughly for every future negotiation.

INDEX

ACKNOWLEDGMENTS

AUTHOR'S ACKNOWLEDGMENTS

The production of this book has called on the skills of many people. I would like particularly to mention my editors at Dorling Kindersley, and my assistant Jane Williams.

PUBLISHER'S ACKNOWLEDGMENTS

Dorling Kindersley would like to thank Emma Lawson for her valuable part in the planning and development of this series, everyone who generously lent props for the photoshoots, and the following for their help and participation:

Editorial Tracey Beresford, Anna Cheifetz, Michael Downey, Jane Garton, Adèle Hayward, Catherine Rubinstein, David Tombesi-Walton; **Design** Helen Benfield, Darren Hill, Ian Midson, Simon J. M. Oon, Kate Poole, Nicola Webb, Ellen Woodward; **DTP assistance** Rachel Symons; **Consultants** Josephine Bryan, Jane Lyle; **Indexer** Hilary Bird; **Proofreader** David Perry; **Photography** Steve Gorton; **Additional photography** Andy Crawford, Tim Ridley; **Photographers' assistants** Sarah Ashun, Nick Goodall, Lee Walsh; **Illustrators** Joanna Cameron, Yahya El-Droubie, Richard Tibbetts.

Models Felicity Crowe, Patrick Dobbs, Carole Evans, Ben Glickman, Sotiris Melioumis, Mutsumi Niwa, Ted Nixon, Kiran Shah, Fiona Terry, Tessa Woodward, Gilbert Wu; **Makeup** Elizabeth Burrage.

Special thanks to the following for their help throughout the series:
Ron and Chris at Clark Davis & Co. Ltd for stationery and furniture supplies; Pam Bennett and the staff at Jones Bootmakers, Covent Garden, for the loan of footwear; Alan Pfaff and the staff at Moss Bros, Covent Garden, for the loan of the men's suits; David Bailey for his help and time; Graham Preston and the staff at Staverton for their time and space; and Anna Youle for all her support and assistance.

Suppliers Austin Reed, Church & Co., Compaq, David Clulow Opticians, Elonex, Escada, Filofax, Mucci Bags.

Picture researcher Mariana Sonnenberg; **Picture library assistant** Sam Ward.

PICTURE CREDITS

Key: *b* bottom, *c* center, *l* left, *r* right, *t* top
Market Photo Agency Inc jacket front cover *br*;
Tony Stone Images jacket front cover *tr*, 4–5, 14*br*, 9*br*, 65*br*.

AUTHOR'S BIOGRAPHY

Tim Hindle is founder of the London-based business language consulting firm, Working Words, which helps international companies compose material in English and communicate their messages clearly to their intended audiences. A regular business writer, Tim Hindle has been a contributor to *The Economist* since 1979 and was editor of *EuroBusiness* from 1994 to 1996. As editorial consultant and author, he has produced a number of titles including *Pocket Manager, Pocket MBA,* and *Pocket Finance,* and a biography of Asil Nadir, *The Sultan of Berkeley Square.*